MIGRAPRENEURS

THE POTENTIALS FOR DIVERSIFYING OUR DIVERSITY

Ephraim Osaghae MBA, MBL, PMP

ISBN 978-0-6484799-9-4

Table of Contents

DEDICATION

To immigrants around the world: I salute you for your courage and tenacity.

To all that make the change worthwhile: I salute you for your big heart.

This is to our success: as employees, as entrepreneurs, as a multicultural world.

ACKNOWLEDGMENT

I want to thank my colleagues at Multicultural Professional Bridge (MPB) and Tri-W Pty Ltd for being part of my journey.

My family has provided me with the balance required to thrive in the face of challenges. My story is not complete without the significance of family.

INTRODUCTION

For reasons best known to you, you've left your country of birth; you've decided to settle in a new country and build a new life. Does that mean you need to lose your identity and value? Does that warrant that you sacrifice your ingenuity and drive for success? Does that mean you need to settle for less in life, with little or no options? Well, you need a change of perception if you think the response to any of those questions is a yes.

It takes time for immigrants to settle into a new environment, especially with a new culture, weather conditions, communities, professional and business environments.

This could contribute to the reasons why they often limit themselves and accept the myth that they have to strive too hard to thrive. But being part of something new doesn't change who you are and your capabilities.

This book is purposed to enlighten immigrants out there who are scared of taking steps to awaken the entrepreneur within them. It aims to inform, inspire, challenge, and provide support in exploring their potentials in the new country. Have you ever thought of owning your business since you relocated (or planning to relocate)? Have you considered this as a viable option or supplement to being an employee? You may be one of the immigrants who think they need to find their place for a few years in the new environment before starting anything substantial for themselves. However, the story does not always end as planned.

Immigrants often commence seeking employment as soon as they arrive in the new country. Some even plan their search even before leaving their home country. Many others have become "professional jobseekers" as they keep writing heaps of job applications associated with an almost equivalent number of rejections and the less obvious negative psychological impacts.

This crazy drive to fit in or establish something solid for oneself has led many to forget the special entrepreneurial skills they possess and can exploit. If you're in this category, then you've found the right book to drive you back on the entrepreneurial path. If you've already found a job as an immigrant and find it hard to 'get your head above the water', you also need it.

This book is primarily designed for immigrants in need of enlightenment, inspiration and challenge in their pursuit of self-actualization and financial freedom. However, all stakeholders, such as locals, educators, members of chambers of commerce and industry, governmental bodies, etc., can also tap into the wealth of knowledge, frameworks, and cultural intelligence therein.

Part of what we're going to discuss will involve getting yourself out of the rat race. It's high time you learned that you have more options running your show instead of joining the crowd and getting yourself entangled and lost working for someone else, especially if that is not meant for you, or it is not working for you, anyway. This book promotes and celebrates Migrapreneurs.

About Migrapreneurs

Migrapreneurs are immigrants who possess entrepreneurial skills and are willing to act on them. It is primarily based on the mantra, "Give a man (or a woman) a fish and you feed him for a day. Teach a man (or a woman) to fish and you feed him for a lifetime." And stretching it further: "What about supporting the man to own a pond containing the fishes?" Entrepreneurship mostly involves setting up businesses, taking on financial risks (hopefully calculated) in the hope of making profits.

This book shows you that you can do this as well, as an immigrant, maybe even better. It is about taking control of your financial status and overall destiny rather than let others and the system decide it for you. Moreover, most host governments want you to succeed; that means more national wealth and economic development for the country as well.

You shouldn't hope to gain much out of this book if you've already closed your mind to exploring a territory that most immigrants can't seem to locate. Open-mindedness is vital in being successful as an entrepreneur. At the end of this book, your view of everything about your "immigrant" status and entrepreneurship will be enriched. You will begin to see several ways you can expand your horizons as a Migrapreneur. So, fasten your seatbelt; it's going to be a bumpy but valuable ride!

CHAPTER 1

NEW HOME, NEW OPPORTUNITIES

The Immigration Narrative

The subject matter of immigration has increasingly caused tension amongst various stakeholders. The reason for this "unease" is far too complex for the scope of this book. However, it will be unreal to avoid including aspects of the narrative that are relevant to the context of this book.

Firstly, it's critical to know that immigration is governed by the applicable law in different countries and jurisdictions.

The decisions regarding matters of immigration are ultimately based on the applicable laws and not necessarily driven by logic or emotions. Such laws will even specify who is qualified to provide migration advice and services. Know the law applicable to your new or intended county of residence. Otherwise, talk to someone that knows. It can make a lot of difference in your immigration experiences. Knowledge is power!

Secondly, let's revisit the question: *Who is an immigrant?* This in itself can generate debate and confusion, if allowed. An immigrant is a person who was born overseas, and whose usual residence is now in another country.[1] A person, according to this definition, is regarded as a usual resident if they have been (or are expected to be) residing in the new country for 12 months or more.

Let us consider the Australian context as a case study. Immigrants born in England continued to be the largest group of overseas-born residents,[2] accounting for 3.9% of Australia's total population at 30 June 2019. This is followed by immigrants born in China (2.7%), India (2.6%), New Zealand (2.2%), the Philippines (1.2%) and Vietnam (1.0%). South Africa is the only

---

[1] Glossary of ABS Report 3415.0 - Migrant Data Matrices, 2012 (http://www.abs.gov.au)

[2] Migration, Australia, 2018-19 (cat. no. 3412.0) (http://www.abs.gov.au)

country in Africa to make the top ten with 0.8%. The remaining three are Italy (0.7%), Malaysia (0.7%), and Sri Lanka (0.6%). These are just a few of the nations represented in the Australian cultural diversity. Can you imagine the potential benefits, if well harnessed?

Opportunities Abound

Immigration can provide a key driver for cultural diversity and the resulting benefits for all stakeholders – government, communities, businesses, people, immigrants, etc. It is like bringing the best from every country represented into the new country. Yes, it is a fact that the sum of the parts may not necessarily result in the best whole.

The issue is whether the inherent capacity in our diversity is being recognized in the first instance. Thereafter, we can confront the challenge of how to further articulate, build, and exploit this value to the maximum benefits of all stakeholders. That's the solution-focus of this book: providing the inspiration and trigger for entrepreneurship. But it starts with that appreciation of the opportunities in our diversity, the enabling environment, and the freedom to take advantage of all these for one's betterment and posterity.

It does not take much time for new immigrants to see the relatively higher standard of living in many countries in the west. The higher quality of transport, health, education, utility, and waste management systems is unmistakable in most cases. The contrast will be more obvious for people coming from poorer regions of the world. This part of the change and experience can be quite refreshing for newcomers.

The welfare system is another aspect that presents significant opportunities for immigrants. The government provides safety nets to members of the community especially financial and social support regarding the risks of experiencing shortfalls in the basics of life. Using the classical Maslow's hierarchy of needs (see Figure 1 below), such support will enable residents to meet the needs of food, shelter (basic), safety, etc.

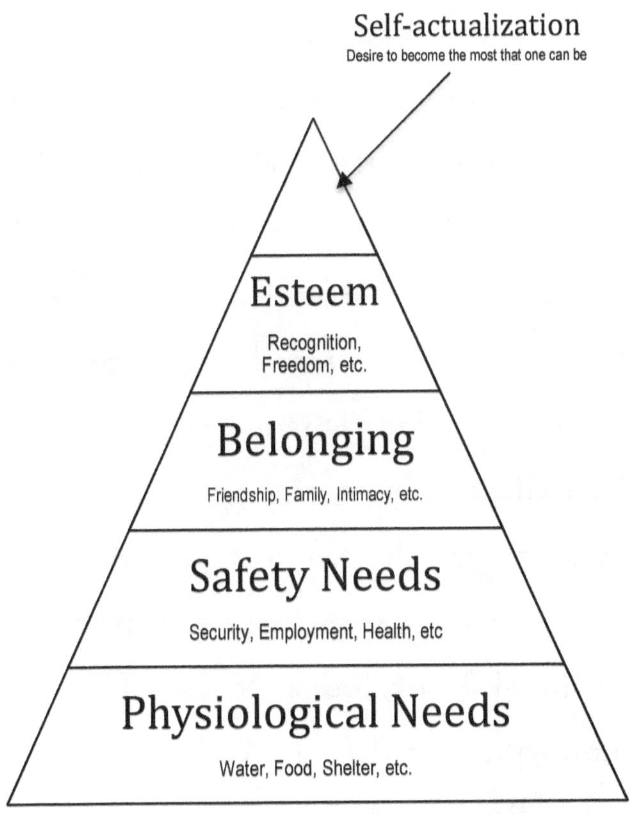

Figure 1: Maslow's Hierarchy of Needs

In Australia, for example, this is done via the tax system and they are mostly means-tested: only those that do not have the means are expected to get the welfare support. Thus, a resident without a job could be provided with a regular stipend while he or she is searching or up-skilling for the next job. This is just one example of welfare support, and possibly the most relevant in the context of this book. Unfortunately, such support (opportunity) could also become a "curse" for many immigrants as they get hooked with such immediate gratification, to the detriment of loftier life goals.

The diversity, the enabling environment, and the welfare safety-nets describe in the previous sections were meant to be a means to ends, and not ends in themselves. Unfortunately, it has become the latter for many immigrants, for various reasons. The motivation to aspire higher and pursue their big goals towards self-esteem and self-actualization (see the upper section of Figure 1 above) may have been traded for short-term benefits, with significant consequences. Now, this is not stating that people, including immigrants, should not tap into the welfare system. There should be no shame in that, everyone has, or will, enjoy the benefits, one way or the other. This is one of the differentiating hallmarks of a good government/leadership where the vulnerable in our society are shielded from the negative elements of life. Indeed, it is not surprising that countries with the right balance will keep attracting high-worth immigrants looking for viable places for relocation and permanent residence.

The call-out of this book is primarily for immigrants with great goals and aspirations to break free of such overdependence. Your success is not just for you alone, it was always meant to bless many more - directly or indirectly. Keep working towards your higher goals because of these opportunities, not allowing them to derail you. Pursue your dreams via employment and grow therein, if that's for you. But if you've always been carved out for entrepreneurship, please do it.

Immigrants often think that they have to depend on their academic qualifications to get them a job, which is a logical starting point. However, have you, as an immigrant, ever paused to think about the traffic of other immigrants and locals hoping to secure employment like you in that same country? According to a report by world migration in 2020,[3] over 258 million individuals in the globe don't live in their birth country, and that's about 3.4% of the world's population. Among those 258 million people, 150.3 million are known to be of active working age, actively working, or seeking work! That is a lot of people chasing relatively fewer opportunities.

Moreover, most newcomers settle in big cities where the competition for employment is even higher. Thus, they

____

[3] https://migrationdataportal.org/infographic/overview-international-migrant-population

stand a very slim chance of securing professional jobs of their aspirations, however highly skilled. They end up doing "survival jobs" which the locals mostly don't want to do. The reality is that even such jobs are becoming scarcer as well. Thus, skilled immigrants are falling back on the same welfare system, sometimes, over a longer period than envisaged.

It's rare for an immigrant to relocate to a new country, apply for a job of choice, and get it. Even when eventually employed, the next challenge is keeping the job without hassles, over and above the typical. If the job is ended for one reason or the other (project completion, product or service discontinuity, redundancy, or termination), how does the immigrant start the process all over again? For some, it could become so tiring and the situation could be contributing to the stagnation in the immigration narrative.

It is unfruitful to be quick in blaming anyone or the system for the situation; it is what it is. Yes, governments and relevant key stakeholders are expected to keep bridging the gaps, and I think they put in their best efforts. However, the responsibility ultimately rests with the immigrant to take necessary steps to break off from the vicious cycle of such overdependence and stagnation. Entrepreneurship is a viable option.

Freedom from Stagnation and Overdependence

Starting from the decision to immigrate, to integrating into the new country, the required change and actions for a better life will ultimately be driven by the immigrant himself or herself. This is particularly the case if higher-level goals are to be achieved.

Have you, as a newcomer, ever considered exploring and exploiting the new environment for entrepreneurial opportunities rather than let the popular narrative and employment trends swallow you up? These are questions you should be asking reflectively and challenging yourself to push forward rather than playing it safe and accepting whatever the system offers.

The reality is that immigrants often possess entrepreneurial skills. They have previously utilized them, in one form or the other, while in their home countries. But they are now scared of getting sidelined if they apply these capabilities in relatively unfamiliar territory. It's high time you changed your perception of things. How timely that you are residing in a country where you can maximize the value of diversity, take advantage of the enabling environment, and rightly use the safety net of the welfare system.

Everybody wants freedom, but not everyone dares to pursue it. A lot of people would rather play it safe under the control of someone else than risking everything for their freedom, even their financial freedom. We all like to convince ourselves that freedom is when we get what we need, and not necessarily what we want. However, that is not a complete picture of freedom in this context. We are financially free when we have enough to get what we need for ourselves and being able to positively influence the world around us.

Rick Santorum, a former member of the United States Senate, analyzing the relationship between government and immigrants, said, "In 1923, there were no government benefits for immigrants except one: Freedom!" Considering the level of freedom in your new country (especially in the west), you, as an immigrant, should be eager to exploit this freedom and not just limit yourself to what the system has to offer you. Truly, these governments want you to prosper because that means prosperity for the nations, which has, or will, become your nation as well.

People often feel they are free as long as they feel safe, and they can do jobs, or get welfare stipends that bring something to their tables often. They go ahead and sacrifice personal goals for systemic arrangements that cover food, monthly bills, and sometimes, life-long mortgages. Jean-Jacques Rousseau couldn't have put it better when he said,[4] "There is no subordination so perfect as that which keeps the appearance of freedom." You can't hope to gather wealth or attain financial freedom under such circumstances. You could ask self-made millionaires and billionaires out there if their salaries or overdependence on welfare got them where they are.

Freedom, in this context, always comes with a price. You should be familiar with this popular maxim, "There is no peace without war." Emphasising the need for context: means taking your chance and getting out of your comfort zone to pursue your life aspirations, self-actualization,

---

[4] Jean-Jacques Rousseau, Christopher Kelly, Allan David Bloom (2010). "Emile, Or, On Education: Includes Emile and Sophie, Or, The Solitaries", p.257, UPNE

and sustainable freedom. Of course, you need to do your due diligence, including feasibility studies, etc., but *the battle is mostly in the mind.* Do the battle. Win the war. Make the best out of your diversity. Achieve your financial freedom.

Diversifying your Diversity

Do you know that you have the potential and resources to build something new for yourself? You may have found it challenging to apply your entrepreneurial skills in your former country, majorly because of the lack of enabling environment and culture, the spamming of your business ideas, and the identicalness in thoughts and dexterity. However, entering a new environment with different people, diverse ideas, new perceptions, and resilient skills, you have a higher chance of performing better.

The chances are that most people in the new country would not have the ideas you have, the skills you possess, and the exposure you have. Why would you want to waste such potentials by blindly joining the already-stuffed-up job-seeking crowd, especially if you can embark on entrepreneurship? It often requires a shift in mindset indeed.

As a Migrapreneur (entrepreneurial immigrant), you're already outstanding with the value you possess. According to a study carried out by Dan Kosten,[5] immigrants are generally perceived to be

---

[5] https://immigrationforum.org/article/immigrants-as-economic-contributors-immigrant-entrepreneurs

exceptionally entrepreneurial and innovative. Several countries create unique visas and easy entry requirements just to attract them because they can contribute massively to economic growth. Also, natives would want to work with immigrants because of the potential in such collaborations. Knowing your worth in these contexts should give you the motivation and courage to explore your skills and talents rather than trying to merely fit in with the norms.

See your new country as a home of opportunities. Observe your environment carefully and you will see several places where you can maximize your value of diversity and access to multiple worlds along with the associated opportunities and resilience. Build your own craft while leveraging off your previous skills, work, and life experiences.

Appreciate the potentials in diversifying your diversity and get to work. Generally, people take a lot of interest in things that are done in ways that are different from the ways they are used to. They want to see new stuff; they want to see the ways people from different places do their things. They like to try out new foods and trades from other countries, but they may not be able to spare the amount needed to travel down to those other countries. They want their houses designed innovatively possibly based on templates and lessons from other regions of the world. Thus, they would need to incur the expenses, inconveniences, and efforts to learn to do it or bring in a foreign expert to deliver their requirements. Guess what? You're right there! You can give them that new or innovative thing they want. That's the reason you will see a flourishing of restaurant owners who sell foreign foods, language translators, explorers of precious metals, culture and media entrepreneurs, talent brokers, exporters and importers, and others.

If several immigrants could open their minds and eyes to see that they have a chance at making it on their own than building wealth for others, they'd thrive a lot better.

Entrepreneurs are mostly business owners, not salary-earners. They take risks with the hope of making profits and, eventually, achieving sustained wealth. It's okay to be a little concerned about some risks associated with entrepreneurship, especially when you have some responsibilities that require money, such as family, utility bills, etc. The other significant but often very personal risk involves scenarios where your partner or other close family members do not have the same level of risk appetite as you do. The need for balance and other wiser steps to take in such delicate situations are beyond the scope of this book. Nonetheless, this should not *stab your entrepreneurial prospects to death.*

Let's go through typical scenarios of the Migrapreneurs that have diversified their diversity.

Case Studies

Food Business

An entrepreneurial woman migrates into a new country and settles in a new community. She observes the environment for a little while and discovers that people have limited choice of food that's being provided in the community. So, she goes ahead to consult with a few friends and relevant governmental agencies so as to learn more about the food industry and regulatory requirements. She then decides to give a small network of friends and neighbours a taste of something new by preparing a particular dish they eat in her previous country. She home-cooks a few meals and invites them over for a complimentary dinner. After the meal, she asks everyone what they think about the food, and most of them gave positive feedback about the meal and their experiences. She documents most of the feedback as much as she reasonably could.

On seeing that they relish the taste of her food, she decides to do it again. This time, she includes free delivery for a group of other random friends and acquaintances. From her observation, the community likes her food. So, she pulls together the little savings she could, gets some basic cooking equipment, secures the required licenses, makes an advert, and starts cooking in packs, which she sells at fair prices with free delivery to neighboring houses including those that attended the first dinner, who are now regular customers.

She makes a little fortune out of the small startup and she's now planning to secure a loan to open a restaurant, create a brand, and employ more hands with ongoing growth. Over time, she will be expanding the business, becoming well-known with a strong and established customer base. She's no longer just a Migrapreneur, but a Megapreneur!

Mining Business

This young mining professional migrates to the west with high hopes of securing mining roles right away. It didn't take time for him to realise the painful reality that being a star professional back in your country of birth does not necessarily equate to being a star in the new country. FW months into the common scenario of writing heaps of job applications, he had an aha moment: mining reserves are finishing in my new country while those in my previous one is yet to be well explored and exploited.

So he gets into diversifying his diversity including enjoying the benefits of *belonging to two worlds*. The key mining players in the mining industry in the new country have advance technology, capabilities, and capital for mining operations. But they lack the reserves of natural resources. The reverse is the case with his country of birth: they have massive reserves of resources, but lacked the technology, capabilities, and capital for developing and exploiting the reserves. The potential for diversity his diversity is huge for the immigrant mining professional in this case study.

He made a couple of phone calls and online engagements, locally and overseas. The first set was done to register and commence mining support services in his new country. The second set was part of his correspondence with former colleagues and professional networks to register a local affiliate of his mining support services and re-established his local network.

As envisaged, he provides intelligence and facilitation support for one of the major mining companies interested in exploring and exploiting precious metals in his country of birth. The match was logical and viable: he provides the services that bridged the gaps between the mining company in his new country, the government, partners, and local communities in his country of birth. This makes it possible to do the business in a timely and efficient manner and win, win, win for all parties involved.

Some doubters would say that the above scenarios are better said than done, and that's precisely where one of the big challenges is – the limiting perception. While the case studies may have been presented in a simplistic manner, in the context of this book, the stories are real. Try and check out most foreign restaurants around you and you'll find out that they are mostly owned by immigrants like you. The same with mining support services especially in countries where mining is a big contributor to their GDP. The latter may be less common due to the fact that it's relatively more complex and capital intensive. But it's real. It's happening. Migrapreneurs are becoming Megapreneurs via such courageous and resilient endeavours.

If you think not everyone can open restaurants or provide mining support services, there are several other businesses in which immigrants can take advantage of their "multiple worlds" and the diversity that comes with it. They include language translation, mineral arts, culture and media, talent brokerage, construction works, consulting services, etc. They will present varying levels of complexities depending on the jurisdictions on both sides. The idea here is to have something to offer your new environment that will incorporate the value of your diversity, and this shouldn't be too challenging as an entrepreneur.

By now, you should know that taking your chance to maximize your potentials costs less than missed opportunities due to inaction. Even if you can't afford to start your personal business right away, you can start small and work your way up steadily.

Notwithstanding, you should also know that the journey of entrepreneurship is not entirely guaranteed to be a smooth one. There'll always be risks in business. But like Kylie Francis said, "You will never reach your true potential living life in comfort and routine. You've got to take some risks," it's either you play it safe and keep looking for employment when you are carved out for running your own business, or you can roll up your sleeves and build something sustainable and reliable for yourself as per your gifting and calling.

This chapter is meant to open your eyes to see the diverse opportunities you can exploit in a new country. You should now see the point in taking your place in freedom instead of trying to stick with the crowd. If your current environment is not allowing you to see the opportunities around you, then you definitely can't stop reading at this point. In subsequent chapters, we will look at the key limitations and obstacles that most immigrants face when trying to settle or work on their entrepreneurial skills and activities, and we'll also explore the solutions to them. Let's proceed!

CHAPTER 2

ABOVE ALL OBSTACLES

Niccolo Machiavelli once said, "Entrepreneurs are simply those who understand that there is little difference between obstacle and opportunity and are able to turn both to their advantage." That couldn't be better stated as the truth. As bad as most people see obstacles as hindrances to success, they can also be agents of success. Obstacles are meant to show us that we are trying something out of the norms, and that's much better than trying to avoid it. If you learn to overcome obstacles rather than avoid them, you will progress much faster towards your goals.

Almost every life endeavour has its challenges. Running a business has a fair share.

As a Migrapreneur, you should expect certain obstacles that could discourage you or terminate your pursuit of success. You need to have a very positive mindset about obstacles, especially if you're trying to build something great. People are more likely to accomplish their business goals when they see obstacles as means to attain more experience and develop resilience. Obstacles are not really that threatening once you see a bigger picture in what you're doing and you get more satisfaction from it. Let's go ahead and see some of the obstacles an immigrant might face in entrepreneurship and business. This section also contains some tips and strategies for overcoming them.

Information and Knowledge Gaps

Successful Migrapreneurs do not take information for granted. They would invest time, efforts, and even money to acquire knowledge, and that's because they know the value of information to their business success. But this is one of the initial (and often, ongoing) challenges for new immigrant entrepreneurs: lack of knowledge on how to convert ideas into reality in their new countries. Consider the case studies presented in the previous chapter. More often, immigrants that are interested in the food business may not be aware of the standards and regulatory requirements involved. In some jurisdictions, for example, you're expected to prepare the food in a commercial kitchen (not at home). Of course, the intent is for public health and safety. That's just one aspect, there may be many more hurdles to cross. Extrapolate that for what you'll require for mining, etc.!

As a Migrapreneur, you can't afford to stay in your own small bubble and try to build a business on your own without the necessary information and support. You may indeed have all the skills and talents needed, but you will also need to carry out constant research to enable you to start and sustain your business properly. Some questions to be explored as follows: How does society work here? Would my idea be viable in this place? Where do I need to start? Can I do it in my house (or rented apartment), initially? What are the legal aspects? What licences do I need? What insurances do I need? What taxes should I prepare for? How do I differentiate myself from the competition? How do I finance my business? How do I survive while setting up my business (including family needs)? Who can assist?

The last question is potentially the most important. If possible, try to learn from other entrepreneurs who are doing well in their businesses. There are community and governmental agencies that are funded to provide such support. Their advisory services would either be free or at affordable fees. It is like using one stone to kill many birds; they can provide information, advice, and guidance regarding the other areas highlighted above. Being informed will enable you to stay on top of your game.

Sociocultural Challenges

This relates to the combination of the social and cultural aspects of any society. Every country, state, city, and community have some form of social and cultural norms. You don't automatically get integrated into society just because you're a new immigrant. Yes, you can expect some kind of welcome and pleasant treatment expected from any contemporary society, but don't assume you'll always have the 'love' in business unless you put in some extra effort on your end as well to initiate and maintain viable connections.

It is already challenging enough trying to get used to the new culture and environment. Social acceptance, especially when it comes to business, is earned with certain qualities. In 2013, a study was carried out by a researcher called Emeka Justin on the challenges most immigrant entrepreneurs face.[6] The conclusion of the study states that the most significant obstacles lie in the social challenges. Migrapreneurs will always need social platforms to enable them to put themselves and their businesses out there in the market. It's often much easier for immigrants who have been proactive in

---

[6] http://erepo.usiu.ac.ke/11732/6297

sharpening their communication and social skills.

Culture relates to the collective behaviours and beliefs of a society, people, or even, groups. Thus, Migrapreneurs must develop the cultural intelligence to quickly articulate the prevailing culture in the new country, city, industry, professional groups, etc. where they now call home and want to do business. This can make the difference between success and failure. Arriving on time for business meetings could provide a relatively mundane but relevant example to illustrate this point. For some cultures (especially in the west), it takes coming late for just one meeting to form a negative perception about you and your business. Some newcomers don't even realize the need and courtesy to call ahead if running late as everyone knows that sometimes, *life happens*. Moreover, it is equally important to apologise at the earliest opportunity and provide a brief explanation for the lateness or for not turning up for the appointment at all. Unfortunately, you may never be told that the reason for the cancellation of the next meeting was because of that singular *socio-cultural error*. This is just one example, and maybe the most relatable. There are many more and sometimes, complex socio-cultural aspects that affect everyday business decisions.

Migrapreneurs, beware and be wise! Take time to learn and appreciate the culture of your new country. The author has another book that dealt extensively with the subject matter of value-add integration: *Adopt Adapt Achieve: An Amazing Triple-A Guide for Successful Relocation, Change and Integration.* Though employment was the main contexts for the book, the principles are applicable to entrepreneurship and business as well. Adopt the new culture as much as necessary without losing your identity. This is now your home and you want to do business and thrive here. Moreover, you're the one coming into the country; it is expected that you'll do more shifting. The need to adapt fast and efficiently is critical to succeeding as a Migrapreneur.

Financial Challenges

Unless you came from your country of birth as an already 'rich' entrepreneur, you might have some financial complications that could discourage you from either starting or establishing your brand. You'll require the fund to undertake feasibility studies and business plan development, securing industry, professional and professional registrations, staffing, embarking on required up-skilling, securing insurances, paying for rent, and so on.

You can apply for bank loans. But the time and effort it takes to secure a good deal of money may be too long and might leave you inactive and financially crippled by the time you've gathered all the requirements. Moreover, the process for securing bank loans will also require you to have properties, etc. that you can offer as collateral. All these economic and financial barriers often make some promising entrepreneurs back off from even starting a business in the first instance. Also, for those who successfully start their businesses, obstacles such as high ongoing rental fees, taxes, and other business costs might pose additional financial challenges.

The great news is that you can start small and grow from there! That's better than not starting at all. Some initial costs cannot be avoided including those for feasibility studies and business plan, business and professional registrations, insurances, etc. However, you can do without staffing and up-skilling for a while. Thankfully, there are cheaper options for outsourcing work these days. Finally, and possibly, most cost-saving measure, you can start from home rather than paying for office rent. Again, this will depend on local industry and government regulations.

Exploring available government grants and business development incentives is one other option for overcoming financial challenges. Some governments regularly scout for great business ideas to fund. They particularly look out for those with an innovative edge, those that can reduce environmental challenges, and those with potential ripple effects including contributing to growth in multiple sectors. They are usually very competitive, but regularly available to explore.

Communication

Brian Tracy once said, "Your ability to communicate with others will account for fully 85% of your success in your business and in your life." That's a very provocative statement! But thinking through even when selecting to share the quote here, I felt it makes some sense. For a start, overcoming all other challenges highlighted in this chapter will require your ability to communicate. Indeed, you might want to ensure you sharpen your communication skills if you wish to thrive at your business in any new terrain. Migrapreneurs would need to be able to speak and understand others in securing good deals and staying strong in the market. If you learn to communicate effectively, you will rarely encounter obstacles that are too tough to handle. Interestingly, effective communication can save you tons of money in several ways. It gives you the opportunity to level all playing fields and eliminate the feeling of being a stranger.

The author has written and worked a lot to try and bridge communication gaps for skilled immigrants along with the issues of lack of acceptable qualifications, lack of work experience, and lack of viable networks. These barriers are also applicable in the context of entrepreneurship and sustaining businesses.

Your lack of ability (and capacity) to speak the local 'lingo' will quickly differentiate (and unfortunately, isolate) you as the 'other' even in business transactions. Just like employment, people generally do business with who they are more comfortable with unless they have no choice but to patronize you, irrespective of your background and affiliations. Trading in products and services related to health and food, for example, will likely experience fewer communication barriers. They are higher in demand and essentiality. People just want good food and care. It matters less to them who's on the other side of the transaction, as long as the standards are there. This is not the case for many other business types that will typically involve layers of selling, impression management, pre-qualifications, competitive bids, soft and hard assessments, even before the final decision to trade.

Migrapreneurs will compete for business opportunities and clients with the natives and existing players that have spoken the same 'language' over the years. They would be required to learn fast and close the gaps. Often, it is more than just speaking the English language. It's also about the local style, verbals and nonverbals, the norms, etc. Communication is king!

Qualifications / Licenses

Qualifications in business contexts relate to the need to obtain and maintain the necessary licenses to operate. This could be at professional, business, and industry levels. Even the locals are often struggling to catch up with the required licenses. Many of them give up in the process. Imagine how daunting it could be for a Migrapreneur. Again, let your vision and appetite for greatness keep driving you to overcome the barriers. Typically, the system in the west is straightforward and prescriptive: undertake and complete the specified steps and requirements, you will have the licences.

Experience

The ability to demonstrate successful delivery of previous contracts and customer satisfaction will be the equivalent of work experience for a Migrapreneur. Potential clients will be looking for evidence of previous projects and assignments that potential sellers have delivered in the recent past. Guess where they will be looking? Local projects and services! This situation presents yet another barrier for newcomers. Great news! Many Migrapreneurs have broken through. Thankfully, the world is increasingly networked these days. They articulate their stories of previous projects and experiences, irrespective of location. In some case, Google maps are remotely used to show evidence along with verifiable references, etc. Ultimately, they are given a chance to compete and they show their greatness within a short period of being tested with a contract.

Networking

Finally, networking is as important to business as it is for employment. The impact may be more with the former, actually. Having a real and potentially viable client base is the key to breaking even, and growth for any business venture. Like they say, "The list is the most important asset of any entrepreneur." Just like skilled immigrants, business immigrants experience the loss of their whole network following relocation. They start all over again to build. That will influence how soon they can succeed in the business.

Reactivate previous networks. As mentioned earlier, the world is a global village. It takes one or two links in a network to get closer to an opportunity. If you haven't, start being intentional with building your local network. Make yourself visible as much as reasonably practicable.

The core of the message in this chapter agrees with the point by Ryan Holiday: "the obstacle is the way." Where there is a will, there is a way. You don't need to fret about these challenges if you can prepare for them as well as having contingency plans. Envisage these potential barriers as part of the risk management framework for your business. Migrapreneurs will overcome these barriers and may even turn some, if not all of them, to their advantages.

The next chapter, which is the last, will help every Migrapreneur, new or old, to learn how to stay in control of their businesses irrespective of all the odds including the ones highlighted above. Even if you haven't started a business yet, you still need to read the subsequent chapter to boost your confidence in how steady you can improve and expand your business. Onward, Migrapreneurs!

CHAPTER 3

STAYING IN CONTROL

We are almost at the end of the line. After all the information and expositions provided in previous chapters, there is a need to instil assurance in the minds of Migrapreneurs. Being able to step up above all your obstacles should have provided some momentum for getting to the top of your game in business.

However, staying at the top requires staying in control. There're sales and margins to maintain, there're competitors, and the ever-changing market conditions remain challenging. How do you remain competitive? There are various management books and research on maintaining your competitive advantages. Below are some crucial tips to consider in the scope and context of this book.

Marketing Strategy

Marketing is one aspect of business that most Migrapreneurs would need to sharpen a bit especially if they want to ultimately achieve the Megapreneur status. Several books have been written on how people could market their businesses effectively and drive sales. However, there is no better marketing strategy than doing what others are doing that works and more. The "more" part makes all the difference. You're an immigrant trying to make a living by converting your skills;

you should always be aware that there are people around you who can easily take up your kind of business too. There is almost no business without competition. Weak marketing strategies won't get you anywhere, no matter how brilliant your ideas are. You need to ensure that your business is viewed differently from other similar businesses in the environment. The idea is to find innovative ways to be different while still maintaining your core value proposition; *think out of the box.* Combine your life and business experiences from your old and new countries and use them to beat the competition. Employ the services of a marketing expert that can gel with your brand and vision while adding value to your efforts and growth.

Focus and Discipline

Commitment and consistency are key aspects of successful businesses. They require focus and discipline. Your choices must be made with intentions. You can't afford to lose your guard for a second, or your entire business may crumble. And trust me, it's not easy to keep starting from scratch as an immigrant. That's the reason most immigrants end up going back to their home country when they can no longer keep up (it may not be better back there anyway). Make it work for you and for your legacy.

You need to set priorities and schedules that favour your business and your lifestyle. It would be best if you found a way to balance your work and lifestyle. If needed, incorporate delegation and stop working solo. Employ assistants, create teams, and surround yourself with people who are capable of help you grow your business. Outsource aspects of the work, as applicable. Use the 80/20 rule to focus more on areas that you can contribute the most value. The latter is more than time spent.

Other things you need to monitor about your business are the traffic rate, conversion rate, profitability, flexibility, standards, and value. That is one of the key reasons to build your business around your core strength and not just doing anything that comes to mind. This will help you to maintain the required passion and productivity. However, you'll still need your focus and discipline to stay in control.

Continuous Learning and Collaboration

Lack of collaboration is another pitfall that has limited the growth and visibility of many immigrant entrepreneurs. There's an urgent need for a shift in this behaviour and narrative. We can be stronger and achieving so much more with collaboration. This is why the author preaches this slogan:

> "If you want to go fast, go alone. If you want to go far, go together. But if you want to go strong, work together"
>
> - Ephraim Osaghae.

Yes, it is wise to carefully select partners and collaborators. Indeed, many great ideas and businesses have been truncated due to wrong partnership. However, that does not entail completely losing out on the massive benefits of collaboration. It's even advisable for Migrapreneurs to explore collaboration with locals in their new countries as this may present significant potentials to leverage off the diversity in such partnership.

Finally, teachability and learning have to continue during your entrepreneurship life cycle. Indeed, it's a common saying that "the day you stop learning is the day you stop living." That is applicable in this context. After all, change in business is inevitable; why would business owners, including Migrapreneurs, remain static? You don't want to become the dinosaur in your line of business, i.e. maintaining the status quo even when the need for change was so natural and urgent. Dinosaurs are now extinct; don't let your business go in that same direction. Keep learning! Keep adapting! Keep being agile!

The entrepreneurial journey will involve lonely parts. There are also bumps along the way. It would require stopovers, refuelling, passengers off and on, and even, long breaks. Doing the tips shared above will help you to prepare, enjoy the adventure, and stay in control all the way. The journey is worth it!

CONCLUSION

Finally, we are at the end of the road! It may be the end of reading this book, but it should be the beginning of reigniting your greatness as an immigrant. The purpose of this book has been achieved if you have been inspired, challenged, and encouraged to explore, start, or consolidate your entrepreneurial journey.

Migrapreneurs is not just a name for migrant entrepreneurs, but it's also a path to financial freedom and wealth building. At the beginning of the book, the promise was to change your perception of immigrants in entrepreneurship, and I'm highly convinced that this promise has been fulfilled. You may not venture into any business immediately; you can take your time to think about it. Even if you have a particular business idea that might be so profitable, don't forget the place of research, risk assessments, and discipline.

The purpose of this book was never to relegate the value of 9-5 employment. The author actively writes and provides support services to bridge employment and career gaps. Rather, this is to highlight the viable alternative of self-employment. Moreover, most entrepreneurs will maintain a hybrid of the two options until they settle fully for one if ever they do.

Now that you get the message, you now know that you can go right ahead and build something significantly good for yourself. You don't have to be dependent on any government or company to take care of you, especially for your higher-level needs of self-esteem and self-actualization. Think of the diverse outcomes of financial freedom in being able to meet your needs, care for others, mentor people, tour around as a positive influencer, and live your best life. You can also leave a great legacy behind. These are opportunities that 9-5 jobs may not easily provide.

You can go ahead and recommend this book to your immigrant non-immigrant friends and acquaintances. The principles in this valuable resource will work for anyone that work them. I hope you look back one day and realize how much it has contributed to your life, either singly or along with other tools. Stay active and never give up! Good luck and Godspeed!

You may also be interested in the
following books by **Ephraim Osaghae**

A
HANDBOOK
FOR
MIGRANTS
The Good, The Challenges,
and The Lessons
Ephraim Osaghae
A Reflective Guide for Meaningful and Whole-Life Experience

A Handbook for Migrants: The Good, The Challenges and The Lessons

A Reflective Guide for Meaningful and Whole-Life Experience

In this book, you will find the following:

- Who really is a migrant?
- The career and business challenges of a migrant; and proposed solutions.
- The challenges and lessons with regards to family life including raising children and youths.
- The essential aspects and preparation for aging and retirement.
- The importance of communities and leadership.
- The lived experiences of a migrant.

You will find great use for the content of this book if you are:

- Intending migrants looking for pre-migration considerations and tips.
- Migrants looking for guidance in work, families, youths and community engagements.
- Non-migrants, students, policymakers, service providers and community leaders.

This book also allows you to participate in meaningful conversations on migrant experiences.

ADOPT
An Amazing Triple A Guide
ADAPT
For Successful Relocation
ACHIEVE
Change and Integration
EPHRAIM OSAGHAE
Author of *A Handbook for Migrants and Voices from Home*

Adopt Adapt Achieve

An Amazing Triple A Guide for Successful Relocation, Change and Integration

Written for all ages and cultural backgrounds, this extraordinary story takes about an hour to read, but the insights can last a lifetime, with knowledge you can hand down to future generations.

This book reveals hard and unknown truths about relocation, change and integration. And focuses on crucial tactics to **Adopt** and **Adapt** to **Achieve** your goals for the big move.

The author of the book writes from two decades of personal experiences and research in relocating from Africa to Australia - the many successes to enjoy, the pitfalls to avoid, and principles for guidance. The narrative includes snippets from his in-depth interactions with diverse members of the community including immigrants, students, professionals, locals, service providers, workers, business people, government officials, and policymakers.

When you know the real stories of real people, you can prepare yourself better on how to deal with change. You can be careful not to repeat mistakes and go on with less stress and more success in your journey even as you consider your family, career and healthy ageing.

Non-immigrants will find useful hints and tips in reading this book given the increasing need for cultural integration in our schools, workplaces, neighbourhoods and communities.

VOICES FROM *Home*

WISDOM FROM OUR DIASPORIC ROOTS

EPHRAIM OSAGHAE MBL

Voices from Home: Wisdom from Our Diasporic Roots

A Narration of Parents of First-Generation Migrants

Every human being is part of a bigger family, which is figuratively represented by the *family tree*. We have roots that extend beyond places and cultures of our current residences. Our roots still weigh a lot into our everyday living irrespective of geographical distance and time.

- This book will provide inspiration, some incentives, and a compass for teachable minds to explore and tap into the wealth of their roots.
- It provides insights on the key dynamics and interplay of cultures, underpinning motivations, and extended family structures of typical first-generation migrants.
- It informs global audiences about lived experiences of people of migrant backgrounds starting with the Australian context.
- It contributes to the value-adding conversations around the themes of identity, cross-cultural intelligence, sustainable migration, etc.
- It provides hints and tips for relevant policy makers, service providers, and other government officials, especially in the areas of sustainable migration.

HOW TO ACHIEVE SUCCESSFUL MIGRATION AND INTEGRATION

How to Achieve Successful Migration and Integration (Workbook)

Turning what could have been threats and weaknesses to opportunities and strengths

The focus of this workbook is to provide practical information and wisdom for getting the best value out of the investments in the big move of migration, relocation, and integration.

The key aspects of migration value chain are covered in the book including factors to consider as part of pre-migration preparations, setting SMART goals, and settling well into your new location.

Learn:
- How to prepare prior to your relocation
- How to transition and settle well in the new location
- How to adopt, adapt and be successful in achieving your goals
- How to sustain the achievement of your goals

Readers and users will learn and receive guidance based on real stories of real people that should lead to real actions for success.

A HANDBOOK *for* MIGRANT YOUTH

PEER TO PEER WISDOM FROM THOSE
WHO'VE BEEN THERE, DONE THAT

LiME Youth

Compiled by Ephraim Osaghae

A Handbook for Migrant Youth

Peer To Peer Wisdom From Those Who've Been There, Done That

A Glimpse into the World of Migrant Youth. A vibrant group of multicultural youth group presents what it takes to make it as a young migrant - to live to the fullest, to achieve your dreams and to enjoy the experience. Prepare yourself for insights, stories and lessons from their lives, and the acumen they have gathered from the LiME Project.

All young people, migrants as well as those who are already established in the new country will find information in this book very useful. And they can use it to inspire others as well.

Parents, mentors, teachers and school administrators will find valuable tips and suggestions in this book that will help them in their ongoing efforts to make great leaders of their children, mentees and students.

The content in this book will also provide government office holders, policy makers and service providers with real stories and lived experiences from young people themselves.

Finally, while Australia is the context for this book, the principles and lessons are applicable across the globe.

TOP INSIDERS GUIDE
FOR
SUCCESSFUL
AND
STABLE CAREERS

How to Secure and Sustain Professional Jobs
Without Losing Self and Value

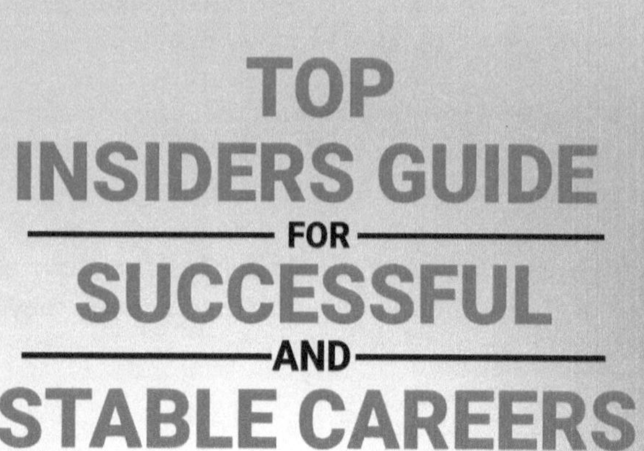

EPHRAIM OSAGHAE
MBA, MBL, PMP

Top Insiders Guide To Successful And Stable Careers

How to Secure and Sustain Professional Jobs Without Losing Self and Value

From two decades of lived experiences (as a skilled immigrant himself, residential professional, and expat work in Africa, Australia, The Middle East, Europe, USA, and Asia, and his extensive NGO work), Ephraim Osaghae addresses tough questions about navigating your new country for successful and stable careers.

He believes that when you learn from real stories of real people and selfless insiders, you can prepare yourself better on how to deal with change, relocation, and other major shifts in life. You can take the necessary actions to maximize gains, minimize pains, and achieve your goals.

This quick and easy-to-read guide book:

- Unpacks the foundational principles of maximizing your strengths, managing your weaknesses, and achieving your goals.

- Reveals master frameworks for communication, qualifications, work experience, and networking.

- Teaches you to understand the critical place of showing up!

While intending, new and relatively more settled immigrants are the ideal audience for this book, non-immigrants and other stakeholders will also find useful hints and tips for job-seeking and cultural intelligence.